The Lac Hong Music Group

Mary Cappellini

PHOTOGRAPHY BY
Marianno de López,
Roger Morris,
and Truc Ly

Rigby

To Chau Nguyen and Mai Nguyen for helping me understand these traditional instruments and to the parents and children of the Lac Hong Music Group for sharing their lives and experiences

THE LAC HONG MUSIC GROUP

Antiem Bui	Tien Nghiem	Van-Thi Tran Pham
Yenba Bui	Minh-An La-Pham	Annie Hong Anh Tran
David Ky Anh Dang-Nguyen	Andy Viet Hai Ngo	Betty Hong Van Tran
Clara Anh Minh Duong	Jennifer Diem Kieu Ngo	Julie Hong Hanh Trieu
Hai Lac	Tammy Tam Dan Ngo	Lisa Hong Ngoc Trieu
Carolyn Diem Chau Le	Michele Tuyet Nguyen	Kim-long Vo
Joseph Quang Le	Nancy Cam Tu Pham	Kimmai Vo

© 1997 by Rigby,
a division of Reed Elsevier Inc.
500 Coventry Lane
Crystal Lake, IL 60014

00 99
10 9 8 7 6 5 4 3

Printed in Singapore

ISBN 0-7635-3130-8

Photo Credits
front cover Marianno de López
back cover Marianno de López
1 Roger Morris
3–5 Marianno de López
7 *top* Marianno de López
7 *bottom* Truc Ly
8–13 Marianno de López
14 Roger Morris
15–16 Truc Ly

Hello! We're part of the Lac Hong Music Group. We're learning to play traditional instruments from Vietnam that have existed for more than 1000 years. Although we were all born in the United States, we love to play these instruments from our parents' homeland.

Most of our parents never had the opportunity
to learn how to play these beautiful instruments in
Vietnam. They want us to keep Vietnamese music
alive here in their new country.

They also want us to learn to speak, read, and write the Vietnamese language. We go to special Vietnamese schools on Sundays. Our parents think it is very important for us to learn about the country our families came from. Perhaps someday we can visit there.

Every Saturday our parents take us to "Little Saigon" in Orange County, California, for our music lessons. We are taught by excellent instructors. They both used to teach at the National Conservatory of Music and Drama in Saigon, Vietnam.

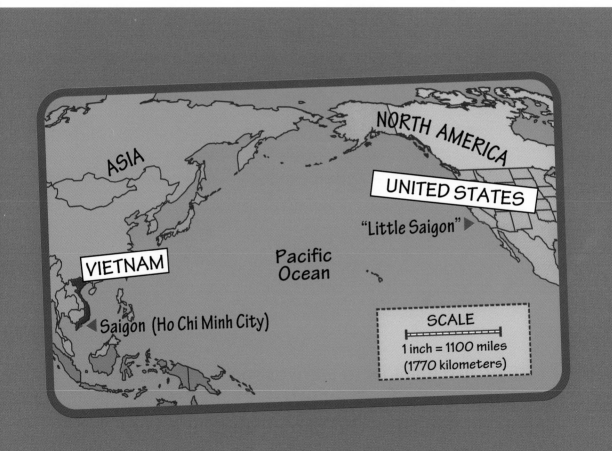

Most of us take private lessons from Professor Chau Nguyen. Then we practice as a group with him for two to three hours. He's the conductor of our Lac Hong Music Group.

Professor Mai Nguyen also teaches some of us, and she helps organize our group.

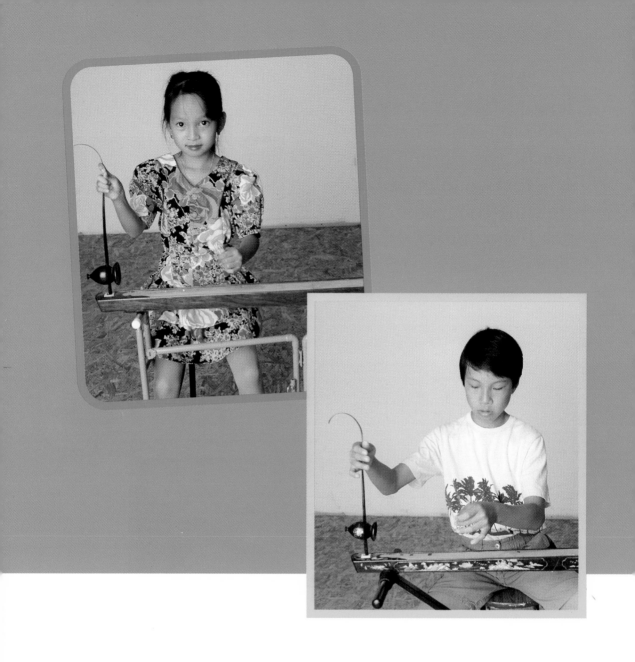

Julie and Andy play the mono-string. To play it, they pluck the single string. They've both been playing the mono-string for two years. It's a difficult instrument to play.

Kim-long plays the two-string fiddle. He holds
it upright and plays it with a bow. Kim-long's
grandfather sent him this instrument from Vietnam.
It has his name spelled out in mother-of-pearl.

Antiem and David play the moon-shaped guitar.
This instrument also has two strings. Antiem and
David play it upright like a banjo, but it's a lot bigger.
It's almost as big as Antiem!

Annie plays the four-string lute. This instrument is also played upright. Annie loves the pretty sound the lute makes and enjoys playing it.

We have twelve girls in our group who play the 16-string zither. To play it, they strum the strings with their fingers. Jennifer and Michele are in the first row. They've been taking lessons from Professor Mai Nguyen for six years.

Lisa plays the 36-string dulcimer. She sits behind it and hits the strings with little padded hammers. There are very few of these instruments in the United States. Lisa feels lucky to be able to play one.

We practice together so that we can perform for everyone in our area. Performing takes a lot of hard work and preparation.

When we have rehearsals, our parents come to help us. They're really involved in everything we do.

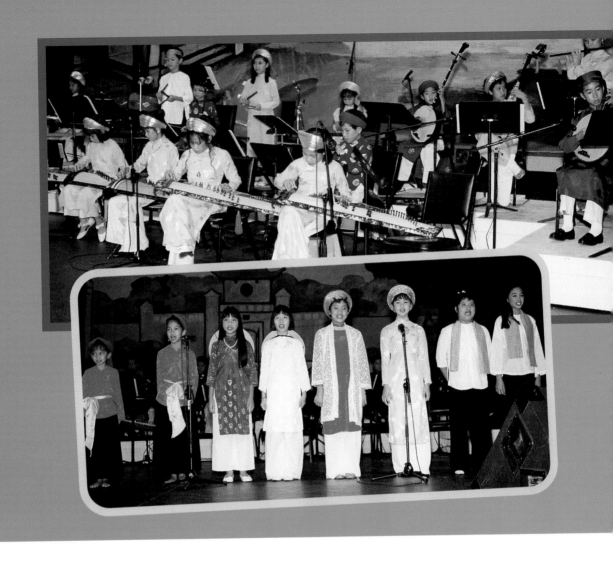

We gave an important performance this year. It was a celebration of the 20 years since the Vietnamese people came to the United States. We played our traditional instruments. We sang a traditional song with pride. Our parents were very proud, too.

We love being Americans, but we also love learning about our parents' homeland. We're proud that our parents are helping us keep Vietnamese traditions alive.